Original title:
Through the Heartache

Copyright © 2024 Swan Charm
All rights reserved.

Author: Paulina Pähkel
ISBN HARDBACK: 978-9916-89-613-6
ISBN PAPERBACK: 978-9916-89-614-3
ISBN EBOOK: 978-9916-89-615-0

Mirage of Forgotten Joy

In the garden where shadows play,
Echoes of laughter drift away.
Colors fade in the evening light,
Whispers of joy take flight.

Memories dance on the breeze's sigh,
Chasing dreams that passed us by.
Fragrant blooms in twilight's glow,
Remind us of what we used to know.

Silhouettes of the past reappear,
Silent songs we long to hear.
Yet in the stillness, hope can gleam,
A flicker of a forgotten dream.

With every gust that bends the trees,
Timeless tales carried with ease.
Each petal a story, fragile yet bold,
In every heart, a warmth to hold.

So here within this phantom place,
We find the joy, the fleeting grace.
A mirage born from love and time,
In a world where memories rhyme.

The Fall of Petals in Autumn

Golden leaves drift from the trees,
Whispers carried by the breeze.
Nature's canvas, rich and warm,
A fleeting beauty, a soft charm.

Crimson hues under the fading sun,
A dance of petals has begun.
There's magic in the cool, crisp air,
As autumn sheds her vibrant wear.

Rustling gently on the ground,
A soft carpet, a gentle sound.
Each petal tells a tale of grace,
The cycle of life in this sacred space.

Moments captured in quiet sighs,
As daylight dims and glory flies.
In the twilight, stories unfold,
Of dreams once bright, now tinged with gold.

And as the seasons turn away,
For what is lost, we always stay.
In the fall of petals, we find the art,
Of cherishing each quiet part.

The Sound of Silent Raindrops

Gentle whispers fall like dreams,
In the quiet, soft it seems.
Pattering on the window's edge,
A lullaby, nature's pledge.

Each drop tells a secret tale,
Of distant lands and a breathless gale.
They dance on rooftops, swift and light,
Filling the void of the endless night.

A symphony of silver grey,
Marking the end of a withered day.
Beneath the cover, hearts will hide,
In the solace where thoughts abide.

Listen close, the world slows down,
While raindrops weave a gentle gown.
The air is thick with sweet embrace,
Every heartbeat finds its place.

Nature sings in purest tone,
A melody we can call our own.
In the calm where worries cease,
The sound of raindrops brings us peace.

Labyrinth of Longing

In shadows deep, our echoes call,
A winding path, we rise, we fall.
Each turn a hope, a dream untold,
In corridors where hearts grow cold.

Whispers linger in the night,
Tracing contours, lost from sight.
The maze of thoughts, a web we weave,
In the secrets that we believe.

Every heartbeat, a step we take,
A journey forged, for love's sweet sake.
But labyrinths with twisted fates,
Can lead to doors and darker gates.

Yet through the haze, a spark may shine,
A glimmer caught in tangled line.
For every longing has its way,
To guide us back, to light the day.

And though the path may feel unclear,
With each turn comes a whispered cheer.
Embrace the winding, feel the song,
In the heart of the labyrinth, we belong.

Embracing the Echo of Farewell

In the stillness, a voice remains,
Haunting whispers, love's refrains.
Each goodbye holds a lingering touch,
A memory cherished, felt so much.

The fading light of evening's glow,
Bids adieu to all we know.
With heavy hearts, we let them go,
While shadows dance in soft tableau.

In every tear, a story flows,
Of laughter shared and silent woes.
An echo lingers in the night,
Embraced by stars, out of sight.

Though paths diverge with time and place,
The moments etched, a sweet embrace.
For every farewell births a new,
A cycle spun with threads so true.

So hold the echoes, firm and tight,
In the silence, find the light.
For though we part, love's journey spins,
In harmony, where life begins.

Dreams Threaded with Despair

In the quiet depths of sleep,
Whispers haunting, shadows creep.
Each dream spun with threads of pain,
A tapestry soaked with the rain.

Visions flicker, lost in time,
Casting doubts in silent rhyme.
Through the dark, the echoes play,
Painting the night in shades of grey.

Yet in the gloom, a spark may gleam,
A fragile thread within the dream.
Through broken hopes, the heart will yearn,
A flicker of faith for which we yearn.

Beneath the weight of tangled fears,
Lie the stories behind our tears.
Threads of sorrow, woven tight,
Create a canvas for the light.

In the midst of despair's embrace,
Resilient souls find their grace.
For every dream, though filled with care,
Leaves us stronger, aware we dare.

Falling Fragments of Love

In twilight's glow, we drift apart,
Fragments of love, scattered heart.
Memories linger, soft and sweet,
Yet distance makes our souls retreat.

Once we danced in a silver moon,
Now silence fills the empty room.
Whispers of laughter cling to air,
Ghosts of togetherness, laid bare.

Beneath the stars, our dreams collide,
But time has turned the tide of pride.
Each moment a thread in fate's weave,
Torn at the seams, it's hard to believe.

Hold tightly to the warmth we knew,
Though fading echoes fall askew.
In the fragments, find a spark,
Guiding us through the endless dark.

Love once bright, now dimmed and thin,
Yet hope resides where hearts have been.
With every piece, I still believe,
In falling fragments, we may cleave.

When Shadows Whisper

In quiet hours, shadows play,
Whispers carried on the gray.
Softly calling, they draw near,
Secrets spoken only here.

Dancing lightly on the wall,
Echoes of the past enthrall.
Flickering light reveals the truth,
A gentle sigh from bygone youth.

In the silence, stories thrive,
Tales of love that still survive.
When shadows linger, dreams arise,
Caught between the darkened skies.

Listen closely, they compose,
Melodies of joy and woes.
Each shadow holds a silent song,
Reminding us we still belong.

As night entwines the fading day,
Shadows murmur, leading the way.
Through whispered tales, we'll find our path,
In shadows' grace, escape the wrath.

Echoes of Lost Promises

In the stillness, echoes drown,
Promises whispered, fading down.
Words we carved in stone and air,
Now linger softly, stripped and bare.

Time has worn the edges fine,
Dreams we wove, lost in the line.
Each vow a thread, unwound in time,
Melodies turned to silent rhyme.

Through hollow halls, the past will roam,
Ghostly sighs of what felt like home.
Each promise made, now bittersweet,
A tapestry of love's deceit.

In the shadows of what we chose,
Regrets blossom like thorny rose.
Yet in this ache, a lesson learned,
From ashes of trust, a fire burned.

As echoes fade into the night,
We'll gather strength, reclaim the light.
Though promises may break and bend,
In scars, we find the strength to mend.

The Weight of Silent Sorrow

In shadows deep, sorrow resides,
A weight that often hides.
Silence screams in muted tones,
In the heart, a silence groans.

Each tear unshed, a heavy stone,
Loneliness feels like a throne.
Carrying burdens, unseen pain,
Lost in a world of soft disdain.

Behind a smile, shadows creep,
A soul so tired, it longs for sleep.
In quiet moments, the heart aches,
Silent sorrow, like a shroud, breaks.

Hope flickers like a distant star,
Guiding the weary from afar.
In the stillness, strength will grow,
From silent grief, resilience flows.

Through the weight, we rise anew,
Finding light in every hue.
Silent sorrow fades away,
And with each dawn, we find our way.

Time's Relentless Journey

Time flows like a river, wide and deep,
Carrying whispers that we must keep.
Moments and memories drift on its tide,
In the heart of the journey, where dreams reside.

Each tick of the clock, a step in the dance,
We move through the shadows, lost in the trance.
Days turn to years with a blink of the eye,
Yet still we chase time, as the days go by.

So treasure the sunrise, the dusk's gentle glow,
In each fleeting moment, let your heart know.
For time's relentless journey will not wait,
To savor each heartbeat, it is not too late.

Echoes of Unspoken Loss

In the silence that lingers, words left unsaid,
Whispers of sorrow, they follow like dread.
Echoes of memories fade in the night,
Leaving behind just a flickering light.

The heart holds these secrets, buried so deep,
In corners of shadows where echoes still weep.
Moments once cherished now lost to the past,
Yet in silent remembrance, the love must last.

Around empty tables where stories once thrived,
The silence is louder, as if we're deprived.
Yet through every tear, a strength can be found,
In echoes of loss, new hope will abound.

Beneath the Weight of Silence

Beneath the weight of silence lies pain,
A heavy burden that falls like rain.
Words unspoken, they weigh on the soul,
Each silence a chapter, each pause takes its toll.

Yet in the quiet, a strength begins to bloom,
A gentle courage emerges from gloom.
For silence can cradle the wounds that we share,
Creating a bond that defies despair.

So let the hush speak, let the stillness unfold,
In the weight of silence, new stories are told.
Through whispers of solace, we learn to believe,
That even in silence, we can still achieve.

Fragments of a Shattered Dream

Shattered dreams scatter like leaves in the wind,
Remnants of hopes that once dared to begin.
Pieces of wishes, now lost in the haze,
Yet flickers of potential still urge us to gaze.

In the rubble of failure, new visions ignite,
From fragments of sorrow, we gather our light.
The heart learns to mend, to stitch and to sew,
In each broken shard lies the chance to grow.

So gather the pieces, don't let them decay,
For dreams that are shattered can still find their way.
With every small step, though the path seems extreme,
We rise from the ashes, reborn from the dream.

The Art of Letting Go

In the silence where shadows dwell,
Memories fade, an empty shell.
Time whispers secrets of release,
Emotions unravel, a fragile peace.

Hands that once held, now drift away,
With every heartbeat, night turns to day.
The weight of sorrow begins to lift,
In the dawn, we find our gift.

Pieces scattered across the floor,
Lessons learned, we can't ignore.
Through the tears, we start to see,
Letting go is setting free.

A gentle breeze through open doors,
Old stories linger, while new ones soar.
With each goodbye, a new hello,
In this dance of life, we learn to flow.

The art of letting go unfolds,
In every breath, a truth it holds.
Embrace the shadows, invite the light,
In letting go, we find our flight.

Where Grief Finds a Voice

In the quiet corners of the night,
Grief whispers softly, beckons light.
A heart once heavy starts to sigh,
In these moments, we learn to cry.

Words unspoken hang in the air,
Yearning for solace, for someone to care.
Through the pain, we start to share,
Finding comfort in love laid bare.

Embers flicker like distant stars,
Healing begins, acknowledging scars.
In shared silence, connections grow,
Where grief finds a voice, love will flow.

With every tear, a story unfolds,
In vulnerability, strength develops bold.
Together we walk through the ache,
Through shared sorrow, our hearts awake.

Life's tapestry woven with tears,
Where sorrow dances with hidden fears.
In the embrace of this aching choice,
We discover where grief finds a voice.

Canvas Painted in Heartbreak

Upon the canvas of faded dreams,
Colors bleed like shattered seams.
Brush strokes tremble, whispering pain,
In the heart's gallery, love's refrain.

Shadows linger where light used to play,
Echoes of laughter now drift away.
Each hue a memory, each line a scar,
A masterpiece shaped by who we are.

Tears become pigments, braided tight,
In every sorrow, traces of light.
Where hearts once soared, now they ache,
In the silence painted, we learn to break.

Beauty emerges in the cracks and folds,
Stories of loss and love retold.
A canvas of longing, yet bittersweet,
In heartbreak's portrait, we feel complete.

With every stroke, we learn to create,
From ashes of loss, rebirth awaits.
In this gallery of what was true,
A canvas painted in heartbreak, anew.

In the Depths of Farewell

Beneath the weight of unspoken goodbyes,
We linger in silence, where memory lies.
Each heartbeat echoes, a whispered call,
In the depths of farewell, we rise and fall.

Tides of emotion crash against the shore,
Waves of longing, longing for more.
In the dusk's embrace, we find our way,
Guided by light of the fading day.

Footsteps fade in the softening light,
Shadows retreat as day turns to night.
Yet in the stillness, we feel the glow,
In the depths of farewell, love will grow.

Embracing the sorrow, we face the ache,
Building a bridge from each heart that breaks.
Through every tear, a promise, a vow,
In the journey of parting, we learn to bow.

In the depths, love's echoes remain,
A tapestry woven with joy and pain.
Though goodbyes linger, they do not sever,
For in the depths of farewell, we find forever.

Beneath the Surface of Smiles

Behind each smile, a story lies,
Hidden tears and aching sighs.
Joy's mask can often deceive,
What the heart yearns to believe.

Laughter dances on the lips,
But sorrow often tightly grips.
A façade that the world can view,
Yet deeper pain remains so true.

In crowded rooms, we wear our guise,
Crafted laughter, muted cries.
The smile shines, but shadows lurk,
A delicate, unspoken work.

With every grin, a tale is spun,
Of battles lost, of races run.
Beneath the surface, life unwinds,
In silent struggles, strength defines.

So take a moment, look inside,
At hidden wounds we all must bide.
Beyond the smiles, the truth remains,
In gentle hearts, we share our pains.

The Weight of Worn Out Pages

Ink has faded, tales grown small,
Time has etched its mark on all.
Pages worn from life's embrace,
Stories linger in their space.

Whispers echo from the past,
Each turning leaf, memories cast.
Thoughts and dreams, now worn and thin,
Chasing shadows deep within.

In the corners, dust resides,
Secrets hidden where time hides.
Each chapter holds a bittersweet,
Life's journey woven in each sheet.

Frayed edges tell of struggles faced,
Moments lost and dreams erased.
Yet within each tear and crease,
There lies a thirst for inner peace.

Still, the book remains unclosed,
A glimpse of strength each story told.
Within each weight of worn out page,
Resides the heart, a timeless sage.

Dancing on Fragments of Dreams

In twilight's glow, shadows sway,
Dancing dreams that drift away.
Fleeting moments, soft and bright,
Whispers linger in the night.

Each fragment glimmers, a lost star,
Chasing hopes that wander far.
Underneath the moonlight's gleam,
We sway softly on the seam.

With every twirl, a wish takes flight,
Lost memories, held tight in sight.
The beauty found in pieces torn,
Reflections of a heart reborn.

Through the chaos, we still find,
A rhythm deep within our mind.
In fragments, love does not depart,
It dances on, within the heart.

So let us twirl on dreams unmade,
In every step, our fears invade.
But in this dance, we find our way,
Embracing night, embracing day.

Canvas of Emotion

Brush strokes paint our silent screams,
Colors burst in tangled dreams.
Each canvas holds a story bright,
A palette born from love and fright.

Vivid hues of joy and pain,
Layered thick like autumn rain.
Every splash, a memory tied,
In art's embrace, emotions hide.

Underneath the swirling shades,
Lie hopes and fears that time parades.
In every corner, shadows dwell,
Inspiration caught, we can tell.

The canvas breathes with every sigh,
A mirror to our souls nearby.
With every stroke, a feeling flows,
In colors bright, our truth arose.

So paint the world in shades of you,
In every hue, let love break through.
For art reveals what words can't say,
A canvas speaks, come what may.

The Quiet After the Storm

The winds have finally ceased,
As shadows softly blend.
A calmness wraps the world,
And whispers of the end.

Branches sway, a gentle dance,
Puddles hold a sigh.
The sky, a canvas washed anew,
Reflects the dreams gone by.

Birds return with cautious notes,
Their songs a healing balm.
Nature breathes in sweet relief,
Embraced in tranquil calm.

The air is crisp, a new beginning,
With earth's rich, scented breath.
In silence, life finds its way,
Beneath the cloak of death.

Hope gleams in rusty colors,
A promise, soft but true.
In every heart that beats,
The quiet whispers through.

Hope Hanging by a Thread

In shadows deep, I wander,
With thoughts like ghosts that roam.
Each flicker of the candle,
Is a whisper calling home.

The stars above, they shimmer,
Like dreams that light the dark.
Each moment holds a promise,
Waiting for its spark.

A fragile thread I cling to,
In the tempest of my mind.
Yet strength is found in whispers,
Where clarity unwinds.

Time drips like melting silver,
A moment, soft and rare.
In the silence, I can find
A steady breath of air.

With every step I gather,
A tapestry of light.
Hope dances on the edges,
Of the long and weary night.

The Stillness of Solitude

In quiet corners, shadows stretch,
Where thoughts begin to play.
The echoes of my heartbeat,
Guide me through the gray.

A single leaf, it flutters down,
In whispers of the breeze.
Each breath a soft reminder,
Of time that flows with ease.

The world outside keeps rushing,
While stillness fills the space.
In solitude, I gather strength,
And find my rightful place.

Memories drift like petals,
On water crystal clear.
Each moment, filled with purpose,
As silence draws me near.

In the arms of gentle quiet,
I learn to just be me.
In the stillness of my soul,
I find serenity.

Blooms in a Raining Winter

The snowflakes softly falling,
A blanket, pure and white.
Yet underneath the surface,
Life stirs in silent spite.

Tiny buds begin to peek,
Through layers cold and gray.
Their colors breaking barriers,
In a brave, determined way.

The world may seem so lifeless,
But hope is shining bright.
In every drop of snow and rain,
A promise of delight.

With every tear that mingles,
The blooms embrace the cold.
Against the winter's harshness,
They flourish, brave and bold.

Life finds its way in seasons,
Though ice may coat the ground.
In a raining winter's heart,
A vibrant life is found.

Dancing in the Storm

The raindrops fall like whispers soft,
In a swirling dance, we find our loft.
Lightning strikes, a brief expose,
Yet in the tempest, our spirits blaze.

With every gust, our laughter sways,
In nature's rhythm, we lose our ways.
Puddles form like mirrors clear,
Reflecting joy, dismissing fear.

Embrace the wild, let worries cease,
In stormy chaos, we find our peace.
For in the whirl, we breathe alive,
Together bold, we dare to thrive.

The world may tremble, skies may roar,
But hand in hand, we crave for more.
An electric bond, forever warm,
As we keep dancing in the storm.

Amidst the Fray of Memory

Dusty halls where echoes dwell,
Soft whispers tell a cherished spell.
Fragments of laughter, tears once shed,
In faded shadows, our stories tread.

Faces linger, both near and far,
In the canvas of time, a guiding star.
Moments collide, both bitter and sweet,
In the heart's gallery, where we meet.

A tapestry woven with threads of gold,
In the warmth of reminiscence, we unfold.
Through corridors of a yesteryear,
In quiet corners, love draws near.

Each heartbeat sings of days gone by,
Carved in silence, like the sky.
Through the fray, we seek to understand,
The delicate dance of hand in hand.

Soliloquy of the Silent

In shadows deep, a voice confined,
Words unspoken, truth outlined.
Silent cries echo through the night,
In gentle sighs, we find our light.

Thoughts like rivers, flowing slow,
Beneath the surface, emotions grow.
A solitary heart yearns to speak,
Yet in the quiet, it feels unique.

The stillness hums with tales untold,
In every pause, a world unfolds.
To listen closely, to understand,
In the tapestry woven, we take a stand.

In the solitude, strength shall rise,
For in the silence, wisdom lies.
A soliloquy that gently sways,
In whispered truths, we find our ways.

The Bittersweet Aftertaste

Summer's sunset, a lingering light,
In twilight's embrace, day turns to night.
A flavor rich, both sharp and sweet,
Memories linger where heartbeats meet.

Like a fleeting kiss, love's warm embrace,
Moments captured, time we chase.
But as the shadows stretch and blend,
The heartache whispers, an old friend.

Goodbyes spoken in hushed tones,
Leaving traces like scattered stones.
In the echoes of laughter, joy remains,
Yet sorrow dances in the veins.

In every heartbeat, a tale resides,
Of laughter shared and love that bides.
A bittersweet song that weaves our fate,
In every parting, we contemplate.

The Frayed Edges of Us

In the quiet dusk we meet,
Whispers woven through the night,
Promises frayed from time's deceit,
Yet hearts still cling to distant light.

Memories swirl like autumn leaves,
Fleeting shadows of what we knew,
Hope, a fragile thread that weaves,
Binding the old with the fresh dew.

Words unsaid linger in the air,
Silence speaks where laughter used to grow,
Through every fracture, we still care,
Navigating paths only we know.

In the tapestry of love we thread,
Stitches of pain and joy collide,
Though edges fray, we're far from dead,
Our spirits dance, their love our guide.

Holding tight to the frayed strands,
We'll mend the seams with hope anew,
Together, carved by life's own hands,
In every tear, a spark shines through.

Healing in the Ruins

Amid the rubble where dreams lay bare,
New sprouts rise from ashes of despair,
Each crack a story, a silent shout,
Whispers of hope that flicker about.

The shattered pieces offer a view,
Reflection of strength in what we pursue,
In the wreckage, beauty finds its voice,
Learning to stand was not just choice.

With every heartbeat, we stitch anew,
Bandaging wounds with morning dew,
The past a canvas of scars we embrace,
In the ruins, we find our place.

As time unwinds its gentle thread,
We weave our sorrows, embrace the dread,
For healing grows in the darkest night,
Like stars igniting the edge of sight.

So let the winds of change blow free,
For in the ruins, we shall see,
A resilient heart, unbreakably strong,
Finding its rhythm, a haunting song.

Embracing the Echoes of Yesterday

In twilight's glow, memories beckon,
Familiar voices wrapped in time,
Echoes dance where shadows threaten,
Embracing all with heart and rhyme.

Each step we take upon this ground,
Leaves whispers of those who came before,
In every heartbeat, their love is found,
A timeless bond we can't ignore.

We sing their songs in morning's light,
Carry their dreams through the misty haze,
In the tapestry of day and night,
Their spirit guides us through the maze.

With arms outstretched to the skies above,
We honor past but live for now,
In every challenge, in every love,
We bow our heads and take a vow.

To cherish echoes, both soft and loud,
To learn from pain, to rise, to stand proud,
Embracing yesterday's gentle call,
In the embrace of time, we rise, we fall.

Waves of Longing and Loss

The ocean whispers secrets sweet,
In every wave, a heartbeat sighs,
Carrying dreams on the tide's retreat,
Soft echoes of love in the skies.

With every crash upon the shore,
I feel your spirit, lost yet near,
A dance of longing, forevermore,
The salt of tears, the taste of fear.

Drifting thoughts like boats adrift,
Sailing through memories we once shared,
In the depths of night, the heartache lifts,
Waves crash softly; I am prepared.

Every ripple a faded trace,
Of laughter and joys, now bittersweet,
I gather remnants, each time and place,
Finding solace where waters meet.

Though loss may linger like a shadow cast,
In tides of longing, I find the light,
With every wave that breaks, and lasts,
I learn to cherish the day from night.

Heartstrings in Dissonance

In shadows where silence grows,
A discordant echo flows,
Broken chords in twilight air,
Love's melody in despair.

Each whispered word left unspoken,
Promises fade, hearts are broken,
Tangled notes of joy and grief,
Harmony lost, seeking relief.

Beneath the veil of starry night,
Dreams collide, lost in their flight,
Fingers trace the scars of time,
A song that once felt so sublime.

A dance of souls, now out of tune,
Once bright their laughter, now the moon,
Plays a tune for the distant past,
An echo of love that couldn't last.

Yet in the dissonance we find,
Flickers of hope intertwined,
The heart still beats in mixed refrain,
A promise that love can still remain.

The Depths of Unmet Yearnings

In deep waters, shadows dwell,
Yearnings rise like a tidal swell,
Dreams that bathe in midnight blue,
Whispers of all I long to do.

Each sigh corresponds with the tide,
Flooded thoughts that I can't hide,
Waves crash gently on the shore,
Longing for what was never more.

Mountains tall with peaks unseen,
Cradling hopes that fade between,
Every echo of a soft embrace,
A fleeting glimpse, an empty space.

Time's tenacity pulls me deep,
Into the void where shadows creep,
Yet still I search, I chase the light,
For echoes lost in endless night.

In depths where fire cannot burn,
Heartbeats echo, twist, and churn,
The urge to feel, to yearn, to strive,
In this vast ocean, I'll survive.

A Canvas of Fractured Memories

Brushstrokes scatter, whispers fade,
Moments trapped in colors laid,
Splashes of joy, flickers of pain,
A gallery of love's sweet strain.

Pieces shattered, yet they gleam,
Fragments woven in a dream,
Every hue a tale retold,
A tapestry of hearts so bold.

Rays of sunlight paint the past,
Ink of sorrow, shadows cast,
Childhood laughter, bittersweet,
Footsteps lost on winding street.

Capturing time in bursts of light,
Memory's ghosts taking flight,
Lingering on this canvas wide,
Reflecting all the joy and pride.

Yet still the brush dances on,
Crafting stories, dusk till dawn,
A mosaic of dreams and fears,
In vibrant colors, laughter, tears.

Reflections in a Tear-streaked Mirror

In crystal glass where shadows cry,
I see the truth that lingers nigh,
Reflections blurred by fleeting time,
A portrait caught in silent rhyme.

Each tear a story, softly told,
Echoes of warmth, whispers of cold,
Fractured dreams upon the frame,
Lives entwined with joy and shame.

Prisms of heartache, light refracted,
Moments cherished, love impacted,
In broken panes truth resides,
Ghosts of laughter, where heart hides.

Glistening memories like scattered stars,
Each one a scar, each one a bar,
Holding secrets, hopes on fire,
Reflections reveal what I desire.

But as I gaze, I find my soul,
In tear-streaked mirrors, I am whole,
For every drop that paints the glass,
Is a spark of love that will not pass.

Melodies of Solitude

In the quiet night so still,
Winds whisper secrets of the will.
Stars flicker like a distant tune,
Singing softly to the moon.

Lonely hearts drift like a breeze,
Finding solace in the trees.
Each leaf tells a tale untold,
Of dreams that shimmer, faintly bold.

Echoes linger, sweet and low,
Carried by the tides that flow.
In solitude, the spirit sings,
Embracing all that silence brings.

A gentle hush, a tender space,
Where memories leave a trace.
Melodies of lost desires,
Awakening the inner fires.

In the shadows, whispers dwell,
A tranquil song, a soothing spell.
Solitude weaves its soothing grace,
In every still, enchanted place.

Harvesting Hopes from Ashes

From the embers, a spark ignites,
Gathering dreams from starry nights.
In the wreckage, seeds are sown,
New beginnings from what's grown.

The ashes cradle the past's despair,
Yet from them rises hope's sweet air.
With every fall, we learn to rise,
Reaching for the endless skies.

Hands in soil, hearts entwined,
In the darkness, light we find.
We cultivate our silent prayers,
Harvesting love in tender layers.

Through the storms, resilience speaks,
Strength emerges in the weak.
Each lost moment, like a riddle,
Bears the promise to the middle.

From these ruins, blossoms bloom,
Painting life where there was gloom.
Harvesting hopes that fiercely burn,
In every twist, a new return.

A Silence That Speaks

In muted tones, the world unfolds,
A language of the heart that holds.
Every pause, a breath of grace,
In silence, we find our place.

Words unspoken, yet they sing,
In the hush, the spirit takes wing.
Glimmers of truth in quiet eyes,
As stillness whispers, never lies.

The absence of sound, a tender thread,
Binding thoughts that go unsaid.
A silence thick with hidden dreams,
In its depths, the heart redeems.

Listening close, the echoes rise,
Through the void, a sweet surprise.
In every beat, a chance to feel,
The silent promise, soft and real.

In this calm, connections grow,
In stillness, love seems to flow.
A silence that speaks, loud and clear,
Inviting souls to draw near.

When Shadows Dance Alone

In the twilight's gentle embrace,
Shadows linger, finding their place.
Whispers of night begin to play,
As daylight fades, the dark ballet.

Figures shift in fleeting light,
Merging shapes in the quiet night.
Each movement tells a story bold,
In the dance where dreams unfold.

Lost in time, a silent waltz,
Where shadows sway without a false.
Silhouettes spin, a gentle trance,
In the murmur of the night's romance.

Walls of dusk, a secret stage,
Painting the world, page by page.
When shadows dance, they find their song,
In their rhythm, we all belong.

Embracing night, they twirl and spin,
In the dance, we find what's within.
Alone yet joined in a cosmic flow,
Shadows whisper what we don't know.

Letters Never Sent

Words unspoken linger long,
In shadows where they don't belong.
Fingers poised, just out of reach,
Emotions lost, too shy to breach.

Ink dries on pages, silent plea,
Grief wrapped in a memory.
Hope rests folded, tight within,
Waiting for a chance to begin.

Each sentence echoes, whispers soft,
Memories crumble, drift aloft.
Letters waiting, never found,
In the void, they spin around.

Frayed edges tell a tale untold,
Promises lost, like treasures of gold.
In dreams they fly, unbound by fate,
Yet still they linger, still they wait.

One day perhaps, the words will soar,
On wings of courage, evermore.
Until that time, they'll sit and pine,
In a heart, forever entwined.

The Journey Beyond Goodbye

A farewell spoken, tears cascade,
Footprints fade where memories wade.
Silent roads await my feet,
Embracing change, bittersweet.

Horizons stretch, unknown and bright,
Chasing dreams into the night.
Every step a whispered prayer,
A beckoning reminder, I am there.

Through valleys deep and mountains high,
I learn to breathe, I learn to fly.
Each heartbeat leads me further still,
Past the ache, toward the thrill.

The sun may set, but dawn will break,
Through shadows cast, my spirit wakes.
In this journey, love will guide,
A compass true, my heart's own tide.

So here I stand, a stronger soul,
With every step, I feel more whole.
Goodbye was hard, but here I find,
New paths await, with light aligned.

The Space Between Heartbeats

In gentle pauses, moments bloom,
A quietness dispels the gloom.
Between each beat, a tale resides,
A secret space where love abides.

Echoes dance within the chest,
A whispered wish, a silent rest.
Time suspended, breath held tight,
Bathed in the glow of fading light.

In spaces small, the world can change,
A shift, a sigh, something strange.
Every heartbeat, a truth unspooled,
Within the silence, I am ruled.

Tender moments, fleeting yet grand,
Connections forged with a steady hand.
In each heartbeat, I sense your grace,
Finding solace in this place.

Here in stillness, we weave our tale,
Through whispered dreams, sweet winds will sail.
Beneath the stars, we share the night,
In every pause, our hearts take flight.

Mending a Fractured Spirit

Shattered pieces, scattered wide,
A heart once full, now hard to hide.
Each crack a story, lessons learned,
From ashes, strength and hope have burned.

Gentle whispers soothe the pain,
In sunlight's touch, I feel the gain.
With every dawn a chance to mend,
The need to heal, the will to bend.

Color returns where shadows laid,
In blooming gardens, new life played.
Fragile, yet a fierce resolve,
In tenderness, the wounds dissolve.

Time's embrace, a soft caress,
Reminding me, I am blessed.
Wings once clipped begin to soar,
Guided by hope, forevermore.

In stitching seams, I find my way,
A stronger self emerges, day by day.
With every breath, I claim my light,
Mending spirit, ready to fight.

Harvesting the Thorns

In fields where shadows stir,
The thorns begin to bloom,
With hands that bear the scar,
We gather what's consumed.

The sun hangs heavy low,
Its warmth a fleeting kiss,
Each prick a tale of woe,
Yet still, we chase the bliss.

Through days of toil and grit,
We find the strength to grow,
In every thorn we hit,
A lesson we must know.

The harvest brought us pain,
But beauty we will see,
For in the sharpest grain,
Resilience grows like trees.

From thorns our hearts will weave,
A tapestry so bold,
In dreams that we achieve,
The stories will be told.

Reflections in a Broken Mirror

Shattered glass lays bare,
A glimpse of what once was,
Each shard tells its own tale,
Of dreams and fleeting pause.

In fragments we see light,
A twist of fate's design,
The edges cut so bright,
But truths are hard to find.

The echoes whisper low,
In corners where we dwell,
What's lost begins to flow,
Through cracks that know us well.

A visage worn and torn,
Reflects what time can't steal,
In chaos, hope is born,
Each scar begins to heal.

Through brokenness we grow,
Embracing each sharp line,
For in the dark we glow,
Our souls begin to shine.

Moments Caught in Between

Suspended in the air,
A heartbeat marks the time,
Between the now and then,
We dance on threads that rhyme.

Fleeting glances shared,
A breath hangs just like dew,
In silence, words declared,
A world that feels so new.

Each moment whispers soft,
Holding echoes of the past,
In stillness, dreams take oft,
Like shadows that are cast.

With every blink, we find,
A canvas blank and wide,
Where memories unwind,
And joys we cannot hide.

Through spaces intertwining,
We gather bits of grace,
In moments still defining,
Our own enchanted space.

Chasing the Ghosts of Bliss

In whispers of the night,
We chase the fleeting glow,
Like fireflies in flight,
Their magic soft and slow.

The echoes laugh and tease,
In shadows long and deep,
While memories like breeze,
Infuse our dreams with sleep.

Through winding paths we roam,
In search of what feels right,
Each step, a heart's new home,
Where fears fade out of sight.

With every yearning sigh,
We dance on silver streams,
A fleeting lullaby,
Awake amidst our dreams.

To chase the ghosts of bliss,
Is to embrace the dawn,
In every heartfelt kiss,
The night will carry on.

Flames of Memory

In the quiet dusk, shadows blend,
Whispers of laughter, echoes descend.
Flickers of light in the corners of thought,
Warmth that the past so tenderly brought.

Moments entangled, both bitter and sweet,
Every heartbeat carries a rhythmic beat.
Flames dance softly, they burn yet they heal,
Illuminating secrets we struggle to feel.

Time weaves a tapestry, fragile and grand,
Faded images slip through our hand.
We grasp for the embers of stories long told,
In the fire of memory, hearts turn to gold.

Yet storms may gather, and shadows may fall,
Testing the strength of this fragile wall.
But memories linger, refusing to fade,
In the flames of our past, a warm serenade.

So let us remember, not live in regret,
For the flames of our memories, we never forget.
They keep us alive, always sparking anew,
In hearts that have known the purest of true.

The Resilience of a Broken Heart

Shattered pieces lie scattered around,
Echoes of love in silence resound.
Yet from the fragments, new strength is born,
A heart once broken, now fervently sworn.

Time mends what once felt far too raw,
Each scar tells a tale, an unbroken law.
In every tear shed, a lesson learned well,
Resilience whispers where pain used to dwell.

The sun rises gently on tender wounds,
Hope springs anew in the softest of tunes.
With courage anew, I rise from the fall,
A spirit reborn, ready to stand tall.

Love may have fled, but it opened the door,
To a journey of healing, to endlessly soar.
With every heartbeat, I reclaim my soul,
A testament living, unwavering and whole.

So here I stand, with heart open wide,
Embracing the pain, no longer I hide.
The resilience of love will guide me along,
In the symphony of life, I find my new song.

Threads of Yesterday

We weave our lives with threads of gold,
Stories of love and memories bold.
Each stitch a moment, a laughter, a tear,
In the fabric of time, all we hold dear.

Colors entwine in a dance so bright,
Shades of our journey, both dark and light.
Threads of yesterday knit dreams anew,
A tapestry woven with shades of you.

In quiet corners, the past softly speaks,
Of joys unbroken and moments unique.
Faded photographs, a distant embrace,
In the quilt of our lives, we each find our place.

With every unravel, a new tale is spun,
New chapters written as day turns to sun.
Threads of yesterday shape who we are,
Guiding our footsteps like a wishing star.

So let us cherish the fabric we've sown,
Embrace every thread, each stitch we have known.
For in this grand weave, with love we reside,
Threads of yesterday weave futures so wide.

The Abyss of Longing

In the deep of night, shadows creep,
Echoes of dreams in silence seep.
A void that beckons with ghostly hands,
Crimson desires on distant sands.

Time stretches thin in a desperate plea,
Longing for whispers that used to be.
In the silence of stars, a heart breaks apart,
The abyss calls softly, consumes every part.

Through the pain, I wander alone,
In the labyrinth of thoughts, I roam.
Every sigh feels heavy, every breath a weight,
Yearning for moments that linger too late.

Yet hope flickers dimly, a candle's last glow,
In the shadows of longing, love starts to grow.
A journey through darkness to find what is real,
In the abyss of longing, we ultimately heal.

So I embrace the silence, the ache in my chest,
For longing ignites the heart's deepest quest.
Through the depths, I shall rise, reclaiming my way,
In the abyss of longing, I find hope's sway.

Rising from the Ashes of Memory

In the quiet of night, dreams fade away,
Whispers of moments, echoes of play.
Yet from the darkness, a flicker ignites,
Hope stitched in shadows, glowing so bright.

Tattered pages of stories unfold,
Fragments of laughter, the brave and the bold.
In the ashes, we find, what once was a spark,
Life's tender glow, lighting the dark.

Time weaves through the threads of the past,
Filling the voids, learning to last.
From loss, a fire begins to blaze,
Resilience blooms in a thousand ways.

The memories linger, yet gently depart,
Leaving their traces deep in the heart.
Each scar tells a tale, a path we embrace,
From ashen remains, we rise with grace.

So here we stand, with hope in our eyes,
Defying the depths, reaching for skies.
Rising anew, a phoenix takes flight,
From the ashes of memory, into the light.

The Weight of an Unfulfilled Wish

A wish whispered soft, on a starry night,
Echoes in silence, lost from my sight.
Heavy like stones, dreams drag on my soul,
The burden of longing, it takes its toll.

Moments slip by, like sand through my hands,
Fleeting desires that no longer stand.
Time stretches out, a canvas unpainted,
A heart full of hope, yet feeling tainted.

Each breath I take, feels wrapped in a sigh,
Yearning for things that seem destined to fly.
The weight of the dreams, I carry each day,
Their shadows loom large, in the light they decay.

In corners of mind, the visions reside,
But the path remains veiled, dreams often collide.
Still, I chase whispers, in the still of the night,
Hoping one day, they'll emerge into light.

Yet through the struggle, I learn to find peace,
In the heart of the weight, there's a quiet release.
Though wishes may linger, and time may delay,
Strength finds its root in the pains we convey.

Songs of the Soul in Dusk

As day surrenders to hues of deep pink,
Silhouettes dance on the edge of the brink.
Each note drifts softly, carried by breeze,
A melody woven with gentle decrees.

Fingers of twilight brush softly on skin,
Awakening echoes held deep within.
Whispers of secrets, the stars start to hum,
Songs of the soul, in the dusk we become.

Moments suspended, the world slows its pace,
In shadows' embrace, we find our true grace.
With hearts intertwined, the silence we share,
In the dusk's gentle cradle, we linger in care.

Voices of memories, rise with the night,
Each thread of our stories, woven in light.
Bathed in the twilight, where dreams softly flow,
Songs of the soul in the dusk gently glow.

Tomorrow awaits with its promise anew,
Yet tonight, let us linger, just me and you.
For the songs that we sing under starlit embrace,
Echo forever, in our sacred space.

A Tapestry Woven in Heartbreak

Threads of sorrow, spun fine with regret,
In the loom of our lives, the pain we beget.
Every stitch carrying the weight of the past,
A tapestry formed from moments that last.

Colors of longing, a palette of tears,
Layers of heartache, stitched through the years.
Each knot a reminder, of love's bittersweet,
A fabric of memories, both painful and sweet.

Time weaves the tales, both fragile and bold,
In the quiet of night, our stories unfold.
Bound by the fibers, we learn to believe,
In the art of the heart, through loss we conceive.

Yet in each tearing, new patterns emerge,
Resilience blooms forth, like a powerful surge.
From heartbreak, we gather, a beauty to share,
A tapestry woven with love and with care.

Though shadows may linger, and echoes may wane,
In the heart's quiet chambers, we find strength in pain.
For in every thread, a lesson we seek,
A tapestry woven, in joy and in grief.

Beneath the Veil of Tears

A shadowed heart, weeps soft and low,
Beneath the veil, where sorrows flow.
A quiet ache, in whispered tones,
In every drop, a hope postponed.

Lost in the echoes of yesterday,
A fragile light begins to fray.
Yet in the night, a spark remains,
A whispered promise, hope refrains.

The weight of dreams, it tugs and pulls,
In every silence, longing dulls.
Yet through the tears, a strength will rise,
To meet the dawn, with open eyes.

Among the sorrows, we find a way,
To stand again, come what may.
A heart reborn, through trials faced,
Emerging soft, with love embraced.

For deep within, the pain will mend,
And from the tears, new joys ascend.
Beneath the veil, hope intertwines,
In every tear, a love that shines.

Remnants of a Shattered Dream

Fragments scattered, lost in time,
Whispers echo, a distant chime.
A tapestry, all torn apart,
Yet still it holds a tender heart.

Memories linger like ghostly trails,
In every laugh, the sorrow pales.
Yet in the ruins, beauty gleams,
From ashes rise, the ghost of dreams.

Once vibrant colors, now shades of gray,
Yet hope persists, it will not sway.
With every piece we pick and place,
A chance to find a warm embrace.

In shadows cast by dreams gone cold,
A story waits, silently told.
The remnants call, they plead, they yearn,
For new horizons, for hearts to turn.

And in the silence, strength appears,
To stitch together all our fears.
For shattered dreams can still inspire,
A journey sparked by inner fire.

Navigating the Storm Within

Waves of doubt crash against the soul,
A tempest fierce, losing control.
Yet in the chaos, a voice breaks through,
A whisper calm, a guiding view.

The heart a compass, true and wise,
Navigating storms beneath dark skies.
With every breath, a steady beat,
In turbulent seas, we find our feet.

Clouds may gather, shadows may loom,
Yet hope's light pierces through the gloom.
In every tempest, strength we find,
A resilience born of the mind.

Sailing forth on waves of fears,
With courage buoyed by unshed tears.
Beneath the fury, a quiet grace,
Guides us safely to our place.

Among the storms, our spirits soar,
Navigating to a distant shore.
For every squall that rattles the day,
Brings forth a dawn, a brighter way.

A Symphony of Unsaid Goodbyes

In gentle chords, the silence sings,
Of words unspoken, of fleeting things.
The space between, a haunting song,
In echoes soft where hearts belong.

Each glance a note, a melody,
In the unseen, our history.
A symphony of dreams once shared,
In fragile moments, love declared.

Yet time moves on, like whispers fade,
A bittersweet serenade.
With every parting, echoes grow,
In unsaid goodbyes, the heartbeats flow.

A dance of shadows, twilight hues,
In every silence, our truth ensues.
Where memories linger, softly sigh,
In symphonic strands, we learn to fly.

And though the years may steal away,
The harmony of yesterday.
In hearts entwined, the music stays,
A timeless song, in endless plays.

The Quiet After the Tempest

The storm has passed, the skies are clear,
Whispers of wind, I still can hear.
Calmness spreads across the sea,
Nature's breath, a symphony.

Broken branches, scattered leaves,
A soft reminder of what it weaves.
In silence, hearts begin to mend,
The echoes of the storm still send.

Puddles glisten under the sun,
Each drop holds stories, one by one.
The world is fresh, renewed and bright,
In the quiet, we find our light.

Birds return to sing their song,
In the stillness, we grow strong.
Holding hands, through pain we've come,
In peace, our spirits now can drum.

Tomorrow's promise starts today,
In the quiet, fears decay.
With every step, we rise and strive,
In the calm, our hopes revive.

A Dance of Memory and Mourning

In shadows soft, the past does creep,
Whispers of love, that still run deep.
A melody of laughter and tears,
Capturing the essence of years.

In twilight's glow, we share a glance,
Two souls entwined in a timeless dance.
The rhythm beats with joy and pain,
In every step, a loss to gain.

Every twirl spins a tale of old,
Stories of warmth and courage bold.
Memories sway like autumn leaves,
Each breath a fondness, each heart believes.

From shadows carved in daylight's glow,
The dance continues, we ebb and flow.
With every heartbeat, we find our way,
In memory's arms, we choose to stay.

Though mourning lingers, love remains,
In the dance of life, we break the chains.
Hand in hand, we embrace the night,
In memory's light, our souls take flight.

Pieces of a Distant Flame

In twilight's hue, a flicker calls,
A yearning flame in shadowed halls.
Memories sparked by gentle glow,
Whispers of warmth the heart still knows.

Each fragment shines, a story told,
Of dreams ignited, of hearts bold.
Flickering hopes from days gone past,
In the quiet, their light holds fast.

In every spark, a lesson learned,
Through whispered winds, our passion burned.
The fire's dance in the cool night air,
Guides the soul through love and despair.

Pieces scattered, yet whole we stay,
In the bonds of love, we find our way.
Through distant flames, our spirits rise,
As we chase the stars in endless skies.

In warm embrace, we stoke the light,
Guided by hope through the darkest night.
With every breath, the flame ignites,
In pieces, we find our endless sights.

From Ashes, We Rise

From the ashes, we gather strength,
A story reborn in its length.
With every setback, we take to flight,
In the darkness, we find our light.

Cinders whisper of battles fought,
Lessons learned and dreams sought.
In the rubble, hope takes root,
From the ground, new life will shoot.

Together we stand, hand in hand,
Facing storms that sweep the land.
With courage woven in each strand,
We rise again, we make our stand.

Embers glow with a fierce desire,
Igniting hearts, setting souls on fire.
No longer bound by fear or pain,
From the ashes, we rise again.

Every moment, a chance to claim,
The road ahead will not be the same.
From the ashes of what has been,
We rise anew, our spirits keen.

Pathways Woven with Silence

In shadows deep, the pathways call,
With whispers soft, they gently stall.
Each step I take, the echoes blend,
In quietude, my thoughts descend.

Beneath the trees, in stillness found,
I wander on, no rushing sound.
The leaves converse, a silent choir,
In nature's grip, I find my fire.

The twilight glows, a fading hue,
As stars emerge, I see what's true.
The night reveals a secret plan,
In silence woven, I understand.

Here I am, where paths entwine,
In solitude, my heart aligns.
A tapestry, both vast and small,
In whispered dreams, I heed the call.

With every step, a story spins,
A journey shaped by where I've been.
The silence guides, a trusted friend,
In pathways woven, my soul will mend.

Portraits of Unfulfilled Wishes

A canvas bare, with colors faint,
Each brushstroke speaks, yet none can paint.
The dreams we hold, like petals fall,
In portraits framed, we seek it all.

A wish upon a flickering star,
Yet distance keeps our hearts ajar.
With every glance, a fleeting hope,
In secret paths, we learn to cope.

The laughter fades, a ghostly sound,
In memories lost, we feel so bound.
Each yearning glance, a heavy sigh,
In shadowed corners, our dreams lie.

Amidst the light, we search for more,
Yet find ourselves at closed-off doors.
The wishes linger, bittersweet,
In portraits drawn, we feel complete.

And so we walk, with hearts in tow,
Through tangled vines where wishes grow.
In silent prayers, we find our peace,
From portraits drawn, our hopes release.

Beneath the Weight of Memory

In layers thick, the moments lay,
A heavy heart, in shadows play.
With whispers soft, the past entwines,
In memories held, the silence shines.

Each fragment glows, a tender spark,
Illuminating paths so dark.
The laughter echoes, faint yet loud,
While sorrow weaves through every shroud.

We tread on ground where feelings tread,
With footsteps lost, the stories spread.
The weight of time, a constant guest,
In memories' hold, we find our rest.

An archive rich, both joy and pain,
In every loss, we learn to gain.
With every tear, a lesson learned,
Beneath the weight, our hearts have turned.

And as we walk this fragile line,
In memory's quilt, our lives align.
With open hearts, we carry on,
Beneath the weight, our past is dawn.

Thorns Among the Blossoms

In gardens rich, the blossoms bloom,
Yet hidden lie the thorns of gloom.
A beauty stark, with dangers near,
In vibrant hues, we mask our fear.

Each rose that grows, a tale to tell,
Of joy and pain, of heaven and hell.
With every petal, a story's spun,
In every thorn, a battle won.

The fragrance sweet, it beckons close,
Yet warns of sharpness, no doubt it knows.
In tangled vines, the truth we weave,
With every sigh, we learn to grieve.

Amidst the joy, the heartache hides,
In every bloom, a love that bides.
The thorns remind of what may come,
In blossoms bright, our souls succumb.

So let us dance among the blooms,
Embrace the light, dispel the gloom.
For in this garden, life remains,
With thorns and blossoms, love sustains.

The Rain that Falls in Silence

Whispers soft upon the ground,
Gentle drums, a soothing sound.
Nature's tears, they fall with grace,
In quietude, they find their place.

Each drop a story, light and clear,
Memories held, both far and near.
Through the leaves, they weave and glide,
A silent song where dreams abide.

Puddles gather, reflections flow,
Mirrored worlds where time is slow.
Under clouds, a palette grey,
Life begins to drift away.

Yet in this fallen, silver rain,
Hope arises, easing pain.
With every splash, a fresh new start,
Healing whispers to the heart.

So let it fall, this quiet gift,
In the silence, spirits lift.
For in the rain, a peace resides,
A calm embrace where love abides.

Caresses of the Invisible

Softest touch that none can see,
A breath of wind, a sweet decree.
Echoes linger, faint yet near,
Invisible hands, so kind and clear.

The warmth that wraps around the soul,
Gentle nudges that make us whole.
In the silence, connections bloom,
A tender light dispels the gloom.

Moments fleeting, whispers low,
In every corner, love does grow.
Like shadows dancing in the light,
Invisible threads weave day and night.

In dreams, their presence softly sighs,
A lifting gaze, a sweet reprise.
Cocooned in warmth, we find our way,
Through caresses that softly sway.

Let us cherish what we can't see,
The silent strength that sets us free.
In every heartbeat, feel the way,
These gentle touches softly play.

The Unraveling Thread

A tapestry, both bright and worn,
Each thread recalled, some lost, some torn.
In the weaving of our days,
Patterns shift in countless ways.

Frayed edges whisper tales of old,
Stories shared, both fierce and bold.
As time pulls tight, the fabric strains,
Yet beauty lies in all the pains.

Moments woven, subtle grace,
Through the trials, we find our place.
With every knot, a lesson learned,
In the fire, our spirits burned.

As we unravel, fear takes flight,
Embracing shadows, welcoming light.
For in the chaos, we can find,
A thread of love that stays aligned.

So let the thread unwind and flow,
For in our hearts, we come to know.
Life's tapestry, forever spun,
An endless journey just begun.

The Heart's Hidden Chorus

In quiet chambers, voices rise,
A symphony that never lies.
Beating rhythms, soft and strong,
In every pulse, we find our song.

Each heartbeat echoes, deep and true,
A chorus rich, yet known by few.
Undercurrents, weaving fate,
In the silence, love creates.

With every sigh, a note is played,
Melodies in shadows laid.
Through the struggles, through the fears,
The heart's refrain will persevere.

Moments woven, time and space,
In unity, we find our grace.
Let us listen, hearts awake,
To the music we all make.

The hidden chorus, loud and clear,
Speaking truths we long to hear.
In harmony, with souls entwined,
The heart's own song, foreverkind.

Tides of Unseen Pain

Silent waves crash against the shore,
Each swell, a story never told.
Lost whispers linger evermore,
In the depths, a heart grows cold.

Emotions trapped in hidden waves,
Underneath a calm disguise.
Memories that the darkness craves,
Tides pull back under gentle skies.

A tempest brews beneath the surface,
With every tide, a haunting dream.
Navigating through life's perfect circus,
Beneath the calm hides the extreme.

Resilience forged through salty tears,
The ebb and flow of joy and pain.
In every heartbeat, trace the years,
A journey etched in every strain.

The ocean weeps for what it knows,
In shadows deep, solace is sought.
Though no one sees the burdens grow,
In silent pulls, the battles fought.

The Beauty Found in Bruises

Colors dance upon my skin,
Every mark a tale to share.
With each bruise, a fight to win,
A canvas woven with despair.

These hues of blue, of green and gold,
Reflection of a spirit bold.
In every pain, a truth unfolds,
A story of the brave and told.

Strength emerges from the night,
In every scar, a light is born.
Finding beauty in the fight,
In shadows cast, new paths adorn.

With every bruise I rise anew,
Embrace each mark, they shape my soul.
In hues of pain, a vibrant hue,
Through struggle, I have found my goal.

So let the world see every stain,
Each imperfection holds a key.
In brokenness, we find the gain,
A beauty wrapped in history.

Chasing Light Beneath the Clouds

In shadows thick, the sun seems near,
A glimmer fights through heavy gray.
With every doubt, a flicker here,
Hope chases light amidst the fray.

Raindrops fall like whispered dreams,
Each droplet tells a tale so bright.
Through darkened skies, the sunlight beams,
Leading souls to chase their light.

Beyond the storm, horizons wide,
With courage, hearts begin to soar.
Though clouds may gather, fear reside,
A radiant destiny in store.

We seek the glow that lies within,
A beacon through uncertain nights.
Through every storm, we strive to win,
Chasing that elusive light.

In every gloom, a spark ignites,
A reminder we are not alone.
For every shadow, there are lights,
Chasing dreams we can call our own.

Shadows of Unforgotten Moments

Flickering echoes in the night,
Where laughter lingers, memories dwell.
In silken dark, we hold on tight,
To stolen whispers only time can tell.

Candles burned with fierce desire,
Each flame a name, a fleeting glance.
In shadows cast, we find the fire,
In every heartbeat, love's romance.

Moments freeze, like frames in glass,
Captured sights that softly fade.
In every smile, a gentle pass,
The shadowed dance of love displayed.

Ghosts of nights we won't forget,
In twilight's arms, they gently sway.
A soft lament, a sweet duet,
In every shadow, dreams replay.

Unforgotten, they drift along,
The past enfolds us, warm embrace.
In memories' depth, we find our song,
Within the shadows, we find our place.

A Journey Marked by Absence

In shadows deep, I tread alone,
Each step echoes a silent moan.
The path is long, the weight is vast,
Yet memories linger of a time past.

A whisper calls from distant lands,
While empty spaces grasp my hands.
The stars above, they seem to sigh,
As moments lost begin to fly.

With every dawn, the ache expands,
Carving truths in shifting sands.
I leave behind what once was home,
Forever changed as I now roam.

Yet in the dusk, a glimmer glows,
A flicker of hope, though no one knows.
Though absence weighs, it shapes my view,
And 'neath the dark, a light shines through.

Signs Written in the Stars

Scattered sparks in velvet night,
Whispers of fate, a guiding light.
Each constellation tells a tale,
Of love that flourished, or hearts that quail.

Beneath this dome, our dreams intertwine,
A cosmic dance, your hand in mine.
The planets hum a timeless song,
While constellations right the wrong.

In silence, truths from ages past,
Reflect the moments meant to last.
We gaze above, our spirits soar,
In every spark, we find much more.

The universe writes, with stars aligned,
A map of souls forever entwined.
Each fallen star, a wish to make,
In the dark sky, no heart will break.

When Hearts Wear Heavy Cloaks

Wrapped in layers, no warmth to share,
Hearts concealed beneath the despair.
With every sigh, the fabric strains,
Hiding hopes and aching pains.

The world outside is bright and bold,
While inside, stories left untold.
We walk the streets, our faces masked,
In shadows deep, we're often tasked.

Yet in the twilight, a spark will flare,
A soft connection that strips the bare.
As cloaks unravel, truth begins to show,
We lift our gaze, and courage grows.

With every thread that falls away,
We find the strength to greet the day.
No longer bound by fear's embrace,
We stand as one, in full grace.

The Light that Eclipses

When shadows fall and silence swells,
A moment captured, where darkness dwells.
Yet in the gloom, a shimmer glows,
A beacon bright, as chaos slows.

It dances gently, a flickering flame,
Illuminating all that feels the same.
As night takes hold, we start to see,
That light within, sets our hearts free.

Though chaos reigns and doubts arise,
This light unveils the hidden skies.
With every flicker, we claim our power,
In darkest hours, we bloom like a flower.

So let the shadows come and go,
For in each moment, our spirits grow.
In the eclipse, we find our song,
Embracing light, where we belong.

Stones Unearthed in Echoes

In the canyon deep and wide,
Whispers of the past reside.
Each stone tells a tale untold,
Of dreams abandoned, hearts gone cold.

Echoes linger, soft and clear,
Carving paths we hold so dear.
Beneath the weight of time's cruel hand,
We seek the truths that still withstand.

Fingers trace the ancient dust,
In the silence, we place our trust.
Each unearthed stone, a fragment lost,
Reminds us always of the cost.

With each heartbeat, shadows blend,
An endless road that has no end.
In every echo, a lesson lies,
Beneath the vast, unyielding skies.

So let us gather, one by one,
The stories told, the battles won.
For in the stones, we find our voice,
In their silence, we make our choice.

The Fire and the Ash

The fire burns, bright and wild,
Casting shadows, like a child.
Heat of passion, warmth of light,
In its glow, we dream at night.

Yet as the embers fade away,
The memories begin to sway.
In the ashes, love once strong,
Now a whisper, a haunting song.

Flickering flames bring us near,
But soon the truth becomes so clear.
From vibrant flames to quiet gray,
We find our hopes have gone astray.

We gather close, we learn to mourn,
For every fire leaves us torn.
In every struggle, a lesson learned,
From every heartache, wisdom earned.

But still we yearn for sparks to fly,
For passion's glow, we can't deny.
In fire's heart, we find our wish,
A promised love, a fleeting bliss.

Tracing the Lines of Regret

With every step, a path we draw,
Unraveling the threads of flaw.
Footprints linger, shadowed sighs,
In the mirror, we see our lies.

Tracing lines upon our skin,
Memories haunt, they pull us in.
Each regret, a heavy weight,
With every choice, we tempt our fate.

The heart remembers all too well,
Stories locked within a shell.
Every joy, a loss incurred,
In silent screams we feel unheard.

Yet through the pain, we seek to find,
The strength to leave the past behind.
For every scar, a tale to tell,
In lines of regret, we often dwell.

So let us walk with heads held high,
Embrace the storms that make us shy.
In learning how to face our fears,
We'll trace the lines, through laughter and tears.

The Gallery of Lost Moments

In the gallery, time stands still,
Each frame a memory to fill.
Captured glances, joy and pain,
Echoes of love like soft summer rain.

Pictures fade as moments wane,
Yet still we cherish joy and pain.
Each brushstroke tells a story true,
Of laughter shared and hearts that knew.

Walls adorned with dreams once bright,
Fading softly into the night.
In every corner, a laugh remains,
In every hush, a heart's refrains.

Through the ages, we still return,
To view the sparks, the fire's burn.
In the gallery of lost embrace,
We find our peace in time and space.

So let us wander, hand in hand,
Through memories, both grand and planned.
For lost moments live and breathe,
In every heart that dares believe.

Rivulets of Forgotten Hope

In whispers soft, the dreams once bright,
Fade into shadows, lost from sight.
Gentle streams that used to flow,
Now silent paths where memories go.

A flicker dims in the twilight's glow,
Yet still they linger, seeds to sow.
Through cracks of time, a glimmer fights,
Reviving whispers in starry nights.

The world may change, the heart will ache,
But hidden streams we dare to wake.
For every tear that traces our face,
Rivulets form, our hopes embrace.

As nature's breath in softest sighs,
Rekindles dreams beneath the skies.
With every sigh, a petal falls,
Yet hope remains, in quiet calls.

So let the rivers run once more,
Through valleys deep, on forgotten shore.
With every drop, a tale resounds,
In rivulets of hope, life abounds.

The Path of Hidden Grief

In shadows where the sorrows hide,
A winding path where the heart must bide.
With every step, the echoes ring,
Of laughter lost, a haunting sting.

Beneath the weight of unwept tears,
The road unfolds, revealing fears.
Yet in the silence, wisdom grows,
As every thorn, a lesson shows.

The journey meanders, slow and fraught,
With memories tangled, battles fought.
But from the depths of every ache,
A strength emerges, a heart awake.

Though hidden grief may seem alone,
In company, we find our tone.
For every pulse of pain we weave,
A tapestry of love we leave.

With every curve, the spirit learns,
In hidden paths, the sorrow burns.
Yet through the gloom, there's always light,
The path of grief reveals the fight.

Lingering Ghosts of Love

In corners dark where shadows play,
The ghosts of love refuse to stray.
They twist and turn in silent dance,
Whispering tales of lost romance.

Each sigh that drifts through empty room,
Carries echoes of love's bloom.
A fleeting glance, a tender touch,
Now linger on, they haunt so much.

In every heartbeat, traces stay,
Of moments cherished, now decay.
Yet through the fog of every night,
The ghosts of love still seek the light.

They murmur softly, tales to share,
Of joys once lived, and deep despair.
Though time may pass, their essence gleams,
In every heart that dares to dream.

So let their whispers guide our way,
In shadows bright as night turns day.
For lingering ghosts, they know the truth,
Love transcends age and eternal youth.

Stitches in the Fabric of Time

With needle fine, the moments stitch,
A tapestry of dreams we itch.
Each thread a tale, each knot a pain,
In the fabric where we bind our gain.

The warp and weft of joy and grief,
Interlace through belief and disbelief.
In shades of laughter, tears may flow,
Creating patterns only we know.

As seasons change, the colors shift,
In woven warmth, we find our gift.
For every tear that leaves a mark,
A stitch of hope ignites the dark.

Through threads of love, we mend our seams,
Connecting past with future dreams.
With every stitch, a journey unfolds,
In the loom of life, our story holds.

So cherish each fray, each worn-out part,
For these are the stitches of the heart.
In the fabric of time, we are defined,
With every thread, our fates aligned.

Emptiness in Every Breath

Silent whispers fill the air,
Echoes of a heart laid bare.
Each inhale, a hollow sound,
In the void, I am spellbound.

Thoughts drift like autumn leaves,
Fading fast as daylight grieves.
In the stillness, truths unfold,
Yet the warmth has turned to cold.

Lost in shadows, time stands still,
Searching for a spark to thrill.
Hope flickers like a dying flame,
But I linger, still the same.

Memories slip through my hands,
Like fine grains of shifting sands.
In every sigh, I find despair,
As emptiness hangs in the air.

Yet a glimmer fights to survive,
In this void, I seek to thrive.
With each breath, a chance to mend,
To find the light around the bend.

Lanterns Flickering in the Dark

In the night, a soft glow gleams,
Whispers echo through our dreams.
Lanterns dance on shadows' edge,
Guiding souls to love's old pledge.

Flickering flames, a fragile light,
Chasing down the endless night.
Each heartbeat, a quiet song,
As we wander, brave and strong.

Stories told beneath the stars,
Boundless hopes from earthly scars.
In the silence, secrets bloom,
Lighting paths through darkened gloom.

Threads of warmth stretch through the cold,
Carried forth with hands to hold.
In this glow, we find our way,
Warding off the fears that stay.

Together under night's embrace,
Finding strength in tender grace.
With each step, the lanterns shine,
Lighting up this life of mine.

The Scent of Forgotten Dreams

Faded whispers linger still,
Scents of moments, bittersweet thrill.
In the corners of my mind,
Where the old and new entwined.

Petals fall from distant ties,
Fragrant echoes, soft goodbyes.
Each reminisce, a breath of air,
Scented tales of love and care.

When the moonlight weaves its spell,
Memories rise, a gentle swell.
From the depths of silent night,
Come the dreams that once took flight.

Stardust trails on paths long gone,
In the shadows, they linger on.
In the stillness, I discern,
The lessons that I yearn to learn.

Though forgotten, they remain,
Colors bright amidst the pain.
In the fragrance of the past,
I find strength, my heart steadfast.

Windswept Promises

Drifting leaves on autumn's breath,
Carrying whispers of what's left.
Promises made beneath the skies,
Where love dwells and laughter flies.

In the breeze, our hopes take flight,
Chasing dreams into the night.
Each gust brings a chance anew,
To rediscover what is true.

Through the storm, we walk as one,
Beneath the weight of setting sun.
No matter how far we roam,
In the wind, we find our home.

Echoes call through ruffled trees,
Carried forth by gentle ease.
In our hearts, we hear the sound,
Of promises that still surround.

As the world bends to the will,
Of what fate has yet to fulfill.
Windswept tales, forever spun,
In our souls, we're never done.

Whispers of Empty Rooms

In the corners, silence dwells,
Memories trapped within the walls.
Echoes of laughter, now just shells,
Dusty remnants of bygone calls.

Windows shudder, curtains sway,
A breeze carries tales of old.
Each room a story, day by day,
Secrets in shadows, quietly told.

Footsteps linger on the floor,
Trying to revive the lost.
These whispers beckon, evermore,
Haunting reminders of the cost.

Paint is peeling, time stands still,
A canvas of joy and strife.
Empty rooms that once could fill,
The heart with warmth, the breath of life.

Yet in the stillness, hope remains,
For every end grants birth anew.
Through whispers soft, love still claims,
These empty rooms, a spirit's view.

Shadows of What Once Was

In twilight's grasp, the shadows play,
Whispers of love that slipped away.
Silhouettes of laughter, now in gray,
Flickering faintly as night holds sway.

Faded photographs on the walls,
Captured moments of joy and grace.
Promises spoken during night calls,
Now linger softly in empty space.

Echoes dance in silent rooms,
Ghosts of joy, of hope, and fear.
Their presence haunts with silent tunes,
Filling the air, a lover's tear.

What was once rich, now feels so bare,
The warmth replaced by chilling air.
In each shadow, a story's flare,
A testament to love laid bare.

Yet still we find in shadows' haze,
A flicker of light, a guiding star.
For in the dark, the heart still plays,
Remembering all that love's bizarre.

The Color of Brokenness

Shattered pieces on the floor,
Each one tells a tale of pain.
In hues of sorrow, dreams implore,
The beauty found in every stain.

Fragments gleam in muted light,
Vibrant blues and ghostly gray.
A canvas born of darkest night,
Where hope and promise dared to play.

Lines of anguish etched in gold,
Tangled threads of love and loss.
In brokenness, lives unfold,
Revealing hearts beneath the gloss.

Yet in this array of dismay,
A symphony of strength emerges.
Each scar a story, bold display,
Resilience blooms as spirit surges.

The color of brokenness shines bright,
A tapestry woven with grace.
In each fracture, a guiding light,
Reminding us of our sacred space.

A Journey Through Silent Storms

In the stillness, thunder brews,
A whisper calls beneath the sky.
Clouds gather, absorbing hues,
Of dreams that flicker and then die.

Footsteps echo on the ground,
A journey marked by shadows cast.
In silent storms, we search and drown,
Holding tightly to moments past.

Raindrops fall like memories,
Each one a tear of hope and fear.
Winds carry soft conspiracies,
Of hearts once bright, now barely clear.

Through tempest trials, we must tread,
With courage forged in the night's embrace.
Finding light where once we fled,
In silent storms, we find our place.

As the storm wanes, a dawn breaks through,
Washing away the lingering gloom.
A journey ends, yet starts anew,
In the aftermath, wildflowers bloom.

Finding Home in the Pain

In the depths of sorrow's clutch,
I search for warmth, I long for touch.
Through the storm, I'll find my way,
A hidden light will guide my stay.

Each tear that falls, a story tells,
Of battles fought in silent wells.
The scars I wear, a map of hope,
In brokenness, I learn to cope.

The heartache whispers, soft and low,
Yet in this pain, my strength will grow.
I build my walls, yet leave a door,
For love to enter, evermore.

In shadows deep, there lies a spark,
A flicker bright within the dark.
For every loss, a lesson learned,
In aching moments, bridges burned.

So here I stand, embraced by night,
Finding home, reclaiming light.
In pain, I'll weave a tapestry,
Of hope and love, my legacy.

Shadows Beneath the Surface

In the quiet, secrets hide,
Whispers echo, truth belied.
The shadows dance, a fleeting game,
Beneath the masks, none feel the same.

Ripples swirl on waters deep,
What lies beneath, the soul will keep.
Haunted dreams and fading past,
In hidden depths, my heart, steadfast.

Each movement stirs the silent waves,
In the abyss, I seek and crave.
Fragments glimmer, tales untold,
The shadows grasp, yet I am bold.

I dive into the unknown blue,
Reaching for the truth so true.
Beneath the surface lies my fight,
With shadows cast, I find my light.

From darkness, strength begins to rise,
In hidden depths, the spirit cries.
Shadows may linger, but I'll soar,
To find the light forevermore.

The Weight of Yesterday's Echo

Yesterday's weight, it clings so tight,
Echoes linger in the night.
Memories play, a haunting score,
Dragging forward, nevermore.

The lessons learned, etched in the soul,
In every part, they take a toll.
Shadows of choices, paths once taken,
A delicate weave, the heart awakened.

Yet in this heaviness, I see,
Strength emerging, setting me free.
An echo whispers, soft and clear,
Guide me on, I will not fear.

With every step, I shed the past,
Confronting demons, breaking fast.
Through the echoes, I gain my voice,
In every sorrow, there lies a choice.

And in this weight, I find my truth,
A blooming garden, eternal youth.
The echoes fade, but here I stand,
Embracing life, an open hand.

A Garden of Withered Roses

In the garden where whispers fade,
Withered roses, love's charade.
Petals drift like memories lost,
A beauty marked by heavy cost.

Thorns remain, sharp against skin,
Reminders of the love within.
Faded blooms that once were bright,
Now speak of shadows in the light.

Yet in decay, there's truth to find,
Lessons linger, intertwined.
In withered forms, there's wisdom old,
As time unfolds, stories told.

Harvesting grief, I plant anew,
In barren soil, I find a view.
Hope and sorrow, hand in hand,
Together weaving, life is planned.

So here I stand, among the rest,
Withered roses, my heart's quest.
In every loss, a seed will grow,
From desolation, love will flow.

Milton Keynes UK
Ingram Content Group UK Ltd.
UKHW022118251124
451529UK00012B/588